AF366879

Zia Blizz

FAMILY SAFE TRUTHS
GET TO KNOW THEM

Truths to play Platonically

Family Safe Truths from Truth, Dare & Situations

© Watergies 2024

All rights reserved

All rights reserved by the author. No part of this publication may be reproduced, stored in a retrieval system or transmitted in any form or by any means, electronic, mechanical, photocopying, recording or otherwise, without the prior permission of the author.

Although every precaution has been taken to verify the accuracy of the information contained herein, the author and publisher assume no responsibility for any errors or omissions. No liability is assumed for damages that may result from the use of information contained within.

First Published in **December 2024**

ISBN: 978-93-6356-486-2

PUBLISHING MONGERS

+91 9311101365

Distributed by: Watergies

Rules of engagement

- Minimum players : 2; Maximum players : 10; Best played with : 4-5

- With 2 players, you choose either his team or her team, and ask whatever your team gets. You can both answer the same questions too, if mutually decided, or start over from the other's team

- With more than 2 players, everyone answers every question

- Every player gets to skip a maximum of three answers to questions. NO EXCEPTIONS.

- Go, get to know them without the risk of going too far

Her turn

#1

One weird food that you love

His turn

#2

Most important person in your life

#3

First thing you remember about me

His turn

#4

Best piece of advice you have been given

Her turn

#5

Your favourite vacation country

His turn

#6

One thing you would never do for all the money in the world

Her turn

#7

One celebrity to be BFFs with

His turn

#8

Best prank you have ever done

Her turn

#9

One fake compliment you given

His turn

#10

One person you
are most jealous
of

Her turn

#11

Worst gift you
have received

His turn

#12

First app you check in the morning

Her turn

#13

Last time you cried

His turn

#14

Your worst habit

Her turn

#15

Biggest lie you
have ever told

His turn

#16

Ever ghosted
someone

#17

One thing you would do if there were no repercussions

His turn

#18

Three life goals

Her turn

#19

Most disgusting thing you have ever done

#20

Most
embarrassing
thing you have
ever done

Her turn

#21

Last lie you told

His turn

#22

Last time you lied

Her turn

#23

Last time you cried

#24

Greatest fear

Her turn

#25

Greatest accomplishment

#26

One thing to eat
for the rest of
your life

Her turn

#27

Choose a country
to move to
tomorrow

His turn

#28

Ever stolen
something

Her turn

#29

Message on your tombstone

His turn

#30

One thing you could invent

Her turn

#31

One memory you
could live again

His turn

#32

One slogan for your life

Her turn

#33

One historic
event you can
have on video

His turn

#34

One thing you
have done that
you would judge
others for

Her turn

#35

Weirdest conversation you have ever overheard

#36

Weirdest thing
you have ever
said to a
stranger

Her turn

#37

One family
member that
irritates you

#38

One thing you
are excited
about right now

#39

One superstition
you believe in

His turn

#40

Your first concert

Her turn

#41

One tattoo to get right now

His turn

#42

Funniest thing you have ever seen

Her turn

#43

Best phase of your life

His turn

#44

Worst phase of your life

Her turn

#45

Ever pretended
to understand
something

His turn

#46

One animal you would never want to be locked with

Her turn

#47

Something you are embarrassed about being good at

His turn

#48

When did you stop believing in Santa Claus

Her turn

#49

Greatest day of
your life

His turn

#50

Best compliment
you have ever
received

Her turn

#51

Ever given a
fake number

His turn

#52

Give me a funny
nickname

Her turn

#53

One thing that grosses you out

#54

Your top three favourite movies

Her turn

#55

Most you have
ever spent on a
night out

His turn

#56

One thing I do
you hate

#57

Strangest dream you have ever had

His turn

#58

One contact you would never call

#59

Most scandalous text you have sent

His turn

#60

Most scandalous text you have received

Her turn

#61

Scariest moment of your life

His turn

#62

Most shameful
deed

Her turn

#63

Ever compromised morals for money

#64

One unnecessary products you consider necessary

Her turn

#65

Are you a
morning person
or a night owl

His turn

#66

Most
embarrassing
question you
asked AI

Her turn

#67

Most
inappropriate
time you have
ever laughed

His turn

#68

Luckiest thing that has ever happened to you

#69

Describe your
favourite
pyjamas

His turn

#70

One friend you
trust with a
super secret

Her turn

#71

One friend to
end friendship
with right now

His turn

#72

One movie you
are embarrassed
to enjoy

#73

One thing on your bucket list

His turn

#74

What would you
name your
children

Her turn

#75

A funny truth
about yourself

His turn

#76

Worst thing anyone has ever done to you

#77

Best thing anyone has ever done for you

#78

Last text you
sent to your
partner

Her turn

#79

Ever lied to someone you care about

#80

Describe your
dream life

#81

Worst physical
pain you have
ever experienced

His turn

#82

Weirdest thing you do while driving

Her turn

#83

Weirdest thing
you have in your
bedroom

His turn

#84

Weirdest thing
in your wardrobe

Her turn

#85

One word that
makes you cringe

His turn

#86

Best lie you have
ever told

Her turn

#87

Always be overdressed or underdressed

#88

One app you waste all your time on

Her turn

#89

One app to
delete right now

His turn

#90

One thing you keep losing all the time

Her turn

#91

One song to sing
on karaoke

His turn

#92

Your biggest
adrenaline rush

Her turn

#93

Are you like your
mom or dad

#94

One thing you would do If you never sleep again

Her turn

#95

Do you believe in an afterlife

His turn

#96

Last time you
were angry

#97

One business you could start today

His turn

#98

Best conspiracy
theory ever

#99

Strangest thing
you have done to
get someone's
attention

#100

Do you judge a
book by its cover

Her turn

#101

One thing you
would do if you
found out you
were adopted

#102

Ever slept
without brushing
teeth

Her turn

#103

Ever ripped your pants

#104

How would you spend a million dollars

Her turn

#105

Do you pick your nose

His turn

#106

Most drunk you
have ever been

Her turn

#107

Maximum money
you have ever
spent on a pair
of shoes

His turn

#108

Last thing in your search history

Her turn

#109

One thing you
cannot live
without

His turn

#110

One song to
listen for the
rest of your life

Her turn

#111

Give yourself a
new first name

His turn

#112

Most memorable lesson from your parents

Her turn

#113

Hire a person to
do one task for
you forever

#114

Most embarrassing problem you have gone to the doctor for

#115

One thing you think about while on the toilet

#116

Ever let someone
else take the
blame for you

Her turn

#117

Most offensive
joke you found
funny

#118

Ever made a conversation with a non living thing

Her turn

#119

One stupid thing you take pride in

His turn

#120

Craziest thing you have ever done

Her turn

#121

Craziest thing
you have ever
done for a friend

#122

Most
controversial
political opinion

Her turn

#123

Most surprising
thing in your bag
right now

His turn

#124

Biggest failure

#125

Biggest regret

His turn

#126

Biggest fear

Her turn

#127

Biggest
insecurity

#128

Three wishes
from a genie

Her turn

#129

Worst thing you
have ever done
to your sibling

His turn

#130

One murder with no repercussions

#131

One part where you are ticklish

His turn

#132

One thing you do
when you don't
want to do
anything

Her turn

#133

Ever want to be famous

#134

One thing would you do if you were not afraid to try

Her turn

#135

Worst decision of someone in this room

His turn

#136

One thing you
know you need
to do but don't
want to

Her turn

#137

Ever snooped
through your
partner's phone

His turn

#138

One purchase
that was a
waste of money

Her turn

#139

One cloth of
mine you would
want to destroy

His turn

#140

Weirdest thing you have ever eaten

Her turn

#141

Weirdest thing
you have ever
done in front of
the mirror

#142

Weirdest dream you have ever had

#143

Your dream vacation

#144

Most difficult
challenge you
have ever
accomplished

#145

One food to eat every day for the rest of your life

His turn

#146

Your guilty
pleasure

Her turn

#147

Last time you
helped a
stranger

#148

Someone you
wish you had
never met

Her turn

#149

Three things to bring with you on a deserted island

His turn

#150

Smallest tip you
have ever left

Her turn

#151

One thing you would change about everyone in this room

His turn

#152

Last thing you
searched online

Her turn

#153

A hidden talent

His turn

#154

Worst dressed
person in this
room

Her turn

#155

Favourite family member

#156

Most
embarrassing
thing that has
ever happened
to you

#157

One music artist you think is overrated

His turn

#158

One thing from
the past you
could change

#159

Choice to look
like anyone from
history

#160

Choose one
person to have
dinner with from
the past

Her turn

#161

One thing you hate people knowing about you

His turn

#162

Ever sent a
regretful text to
the wrong
person

Her turn

#163

Ever lied to your
partner about
where you were

His turn

#164

Ever got in
trouble at school

Her turn

#165

Family member
would you date if
they weren't
your family

His turn

#166

Biggest
misconception
about you

Her turn

#167

One fictional
character you
would want to
be

His turn

#168

Ever dined and dashed

Her turn

#169

Last time your partner embarrassed you

#170

Choice to change
on thing about
me

Her turn

#171

Wear only flip flops or heels forever

#172

One useless skill
you want to
learn

#173

Rate your look
on a scale of one
to ten

His turn

#174

One job to do
forever

Her turn

#175

First impression of me

His turn

#176

Choose one
person in room
to swap lives
with

Her turn

#177

Weirdest thing
you have done
when no one was
watching

#178

One thing to be always remembered for

#179

Longest you have gone without brushing

His turn

#180

Most sinful thing
you have done in
a house of
worship

#181

One bridge you are glad you burned

His turn

#182

Most childish thing you do

Her turn

#183

Something you never want your family to know about

#184

Ever returned a
gift

Her turn

#185

Last person you
wanted to punch

His turn

#186

Your fondest
memory with me

#187

One thing you
wish people
knew about you

#188

One person to
be with you on a
deserted island

#189

Craziest thing you have ever done for money

His turn

#190

Something that
no one else
knows about you

Her turn

#191

Your phobia

His turn

#192

What do you
admire the most
about me

Her turn

#193

Where do you
see yourself in
ten years

His turn

#194

Choose one
alcoholic
beverage to
drink forever

Her turn

#195

One thing you would wait in queue for twenty four hours

His turn

#196

Last time you
apologised

Her turn

#197

Longest time you have gone without a shower

His turn

#198

Last time you
got caught in a
lie

Her turn

#199

Most
embarrassing
purchase

#200

One question to ask a fortune teller

201

Ever thrown up
in public

202

Should you have secrets in a relationship

Her turn

203

Choose a name for the show if we were a sitcom

His turn

204

One movie that always makes you cry

Her turn

205

One personal habit that would embarrass you in front of me

His turn

206

Worst meal you have ever cooked

207

If you could be
eighteen again,
what would you
do differently

208

One thing you
only do when you
are alone

209

Ever had a dream about someone in this room. Do tell.

His turn

210

One thing that makes you the happiest

211

Your emergency contact

His turn

212

Last time you shared a toothbrush with someone else

213

Most stupid
thing are
attached to

His turn

214

Longest you have ever slept

Her turn

215

Ever gotten blackout drunk

His turn

216

Your most
chaotic age

Her turn

217

One thing in your house right now you don't want anyone to find out about after your death

218

Will you be able
to achieve your
dreams

219

Your favourite show

His turn

220

One thing that scrambles your brain when you think about it

Her turn

221

Satisfied with your upbringing

His turn

222

One movie everyone should watch

223

One habit of yours that not many people have

His turn

224

Most thankful
for

Her turn

225

Do you collect anything

His turn

226

Do you believe in karma

Her turn

227

Cheered up or left alone in bad mood

His turn

228

Choose one year
to time travel to

Her turn

229

One costume you
have to wear
everyday

His turn

230

One person to
be president

Her turn

231

Ever get a prenup

His turn

232

First thing you would do if you were invisible

Her turn

233

Your biggest childhood fear

234

Ever worn dirty
socks

235

Choose one fictional character as your assistant

His turn

236

One thing you
should do but
you never will

Her turn

237

One song playing in the car if you were in a high speed chase

His turn
238
Do you believe in second chances

Her turn

239

One thing you have done that you would never admit

His turn

240

One thing you have done just to impress someone

Her turn

241

One thing you wish you were better at

His turn

242

Ever sent an embarrassing email

Her turn

243

Ever laughed so hard that a drink came out of your nose

His turn

244

Choose one person to never talk to again in this room

Her turn

245

One person in your life you have to give up talking to

His turn

246

One thing no one knows about you

Her turn

247

Love or money

His turn

248

Ever been friends with someone for getting something else

Her turn

249

One thing you do
when you need
alone time

His turn

250

One thing you worry people judge you for

Her turn

Bonus

Something you want to ask

His turn

Bonus

Something you
want to ask